C902545770

KU-783-331

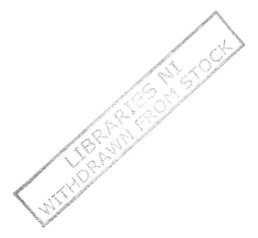

Today is a Hot Day

by Martha E. H. Rustad

raintree

a Capstone company — publishers for children

Raintree is an imprint of Capstone Global Library Limited, a company incorporated in England and Wales having its registered office at 264 Banbury Road, Oxford, OX2 7DY – Registered company number: 6695582

www.raintree.co.uk
myorders@raintree.co.uk

Edited by Marissa Kirkman
Designed by Charmaine Whitman and Peggie Carley
Picture research by Tracey Engel
Production by Katy LaVigne
Originated by Capstone Global Library
Printed and bound in China.

ISBN 978 1 4747 3876 7
20 19 18 17 16
10 9 8 7 6 5 4 3 2 1

British Library Cataloguing in Publication Data
A full catalogue record for this book is available from the British Library.

Acknowledgements
We would like to thank the following for permission to reproduce photographs: Glow Images: Ian Lishman, 10; iStockphoto: Anna Ziska, 16, Christopher Futcher, 4, 20, Maria Pavlova, 8 (top); Shutterstock: blacograf, 14, Aleksey Vanin, 6 (weather icons), Blend Images, 1, 18, goja1, cover and interior design element, hanapon1002, cover, Kseniia Neverkovska, cover and interior design element, Shevs, 12, Smileus, 8 (bottom), vinz89, 6 (thermometer)

Every effort has been made to contact copyright holders of material reproduced in this book. Any omissions will be rectified in subsequent printings if notice is given to the publisher.

All the internet addresses (URLs) given in this book were valid at the time of going to press. However, due to the dynamic nature of the internet, some addresses may have changed, or sites may have changed or ceased to exist since publication. While the author and publisher regret any inconvenience this may cause readers, no responsibility for any such changes can be accepted by either the author or the publisher.

Contents

What is the weather like?

Today is a hot day.

The temperature is high

on a hot day. We want to

know how hot it will be.

TODAY

32° C

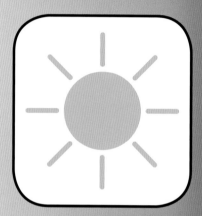

SUN	MON	TUE	WED	THU	FRI	SAT
32°C	31°C	29°C	26°C	27°C	25°C	28°C
(90°F)	(87°F)	(85°F)	(79°F)	(81°F)	(77°F)	(82°F)

We look at the forecast.

It tells us what the weather

will be today. The numbers tell

us the temperature. The numbers

are bigger on hot days.

summer

spring

8

The forecast shows patterns, too.
The temperature can be hot
for many days. Summer has
a lot of hot days in a row.
Spring can have hot days, too.

What do we see?

The sun is often bright on a hot day.

We see the sun's rays. The heat

from the sun warms the air.

The air can stay hot, even on

cloudy days.

We see animals pant.

They open their mouths to breathe.

Their tongues hang out.

Panting helps them stay cool.

After a few hot days, the ground looks dry and cracked. Plants wilt and look like they are falling over. They need water.

What do we do?

High temperatures make us feel hot.

We can get ill if we are

too hot for too long.

Sweat helps our bodies stay cool.

We drink lots of water, too.

Too much time in the sun can burn our skin. We wear sun cream to stay safe. We rest in the shade. Hats keep the sun out of our eyes.

We swim on a hot day.

The cold water feels good.

Can we go swimming tomorrow?

Let's check the forecast!

Glossary

forecast   prediction of what the weather will be

pattern   several things that are repeated in the same way each time

shade   area that is blocked from sunlight; the air may feel cooler in the shade

sun cream   lotion that keeps skin safe from harmful parts of sunshine

sweat   salty liquid that comes out of skin; sweat helps cool the skin

temperature   the measured heat or cold of something; temperature is measured with a thermometer

wilt   to droop; some plants lose water and bend over in the heat

Find out more

Books

Humidity (Understanding Weather), Kristin Schuetz (Bellwether Media, 2016)

Summer (Seasons), Stephanie Turnbull (Franklin Watts, 2015)

Sunshine (Weather Wise), Helen Cox Cannons (Raintree, 2015)

Websites

easyscienceforkids.com/all-about-temperature
Learn all about temperature by reading fun facts and watching a video.

www.weatherwizkids.com/?page_id=80
Learn all about forecasting the weather and find directions to perform your own weather experiments.

www.ready.gov/kids/know-the-facts/extreme-heat
Visit this site to learn how to prepare for extreme heat.

Index

Note to parents and teachers

The What is the Weather Today? series supports National Curriculum requirements for science related to weather. This book describes and illustrates a hot day. The images support early readers in understanding the text. The repetition of words and phrases helps early readers learn new words. This book also introduces early readers to subject-specific vocabulary words, which are defined in the Glossary section. Early readers may need assistance to read some words and to use the Contents, Glossary, Find out more and Index sections of the book.